Taking the Kids

TO NORTHERN CALIFORNIA

Other books in the *Taking the Kids* series:

Taking the Kids to the Great American Southwest
Taking the Kids to Sunny Southern California

Taking the Kids
TO NORTHERN CALIFORNIA

Everything That's Fun to Do and See for Kids—and Parents Too!

Eileen Ogintz

HarperCollins*West*
A Division of HarperCollinsPublishers

HarperCollins West and the author, in association with the Basic Foundation, a not-for-profit organization whose primary mission is reforestation, will facilitate the planting of two trees for every one tree used in the manufacture of this book.

This edition is printed on acid-free paper that meets the American National Standards Institute Z39.48 Standard.

FIRST EDITION

Library of Congress Cataloging–in–Publication Data

Ogintz, Eileen.
   Taking the Kids to Northern California: Everything That's Fun to Do and See for Kids—and Parents too! / Eileen Ogintz
   p. cm. — (Taking the kids)
   ISBN 0-06-258547-9 : $9.95
   1. California, Northern — Guidebooks — Juvenile literature.
   2. Amusements — California, Northern — Guidebooks — Juvenile literature. I. Title II. Series.
F867.5.035 1994   94-21516
917.94—dc20   CIP
                                                                   AC

94 95 96 97 98 RRD(c)   10 9 8 7 6 5 4 3 2 1

To Andy, Matt, Reggie, and Melanie: Thanks for always showing me the way.

This book wouldn't have been written without the help of dozens of people across Northern California. National park rangers, city and small-town tourism officials, museum experts, and California parents generously shared their time and knowledge so that I could make this book fun for all of our kids.

Special thanks to the San Francisco Convention & Visitors Bureau's Dawn Stranne for helping me arrange the logistics. Also to the Museum of the City of San Francisco's Gladys Hansen, who made sure I knew San Francisco's history. Rand Richards's *Historic San Francisco* was a big help, as was Barry Parr's *San Francisco and the Bay Area,* and Ray Riegert's *Hidden San Francisco and Northern California.* I wish I'd had a social studies text in grade school that was as much fun to read as Houghton Mifflin's *Oh California!*

Thanks to Northern California kids Marc and Molly Mermelstein and also to Todd Musburger for his counsel, Steph Meismer for her fact-checking, and Joann Moschella, Beth Weber, and the rest of the HarperCollins crew for making the *Taking the Kids* series really happen.

CONTENTS

SAN FRANCISCO

EARTHQUAKES, HILLS, AND CABLE CARS

The horse pulling the streetcar up the steep San Francisco hill stumbled in the mud and fell. The frantic driver couldn't get his brakes to hold. The crowded car rolled back down the hill, dragging the entire team of helpless horses behind it.

That drizzly night in 1869, a young engineer named Andrew

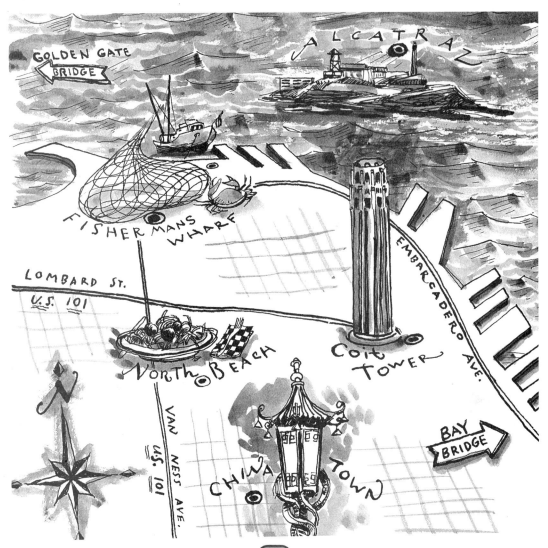

GOLDEN GATE
BRIDGE

ALCATRAZ

FISHERMANS
WHARF

LOMBARD ST.

U.S. 101

NORTH BEACH

COIT
TOWER

EMBARCADERO AVE.

VAN NESS AVE.

U.S. 101

CHINA TOWN

BAY
BRIDGE

Hallidie was horrified as he watched the scene. He decided there had to be a better way to get people up and down San Francisco's many hills. When he began trying to solve this puzzle, he had no idea how much he would change things.

Hallidie thought an underground steel cable could pull the streetcars. He and his father were already making and selling wire rope and he knew how strong it was. Even though people in San Francisco laughed at his idea, Hallidie didn't give up. Thanks to him, the first cable car in the world, the Clay Street Hill Railroad, officially started running on September 1, 1873, and was an

❧ Cable Cars ❧

Cable cars are different from buses or subways. Here are some tips for happy riding:

- Cable cars stop at most corners along their routes. Look for the maroon and white cable car stop signs. Wave to alert the gripman to stop.
- Use either side to board, but be careful of traffic.
- Don't stand in the space between the gripman and the front door. It must be kept clear. The same goes for the yellow floor spaces.
- Face the direction you're going. Don't lean out from the running boards, and be sure to hold on around the curves.
- Tell the gripman or conductor when you want to get off.

immediate hit. Within a few years, cable cars were carrying people all over San Francisco.

Soon, there were cable railways in many cities across the country. But only San Francisco's cable cars are still running. Today's shiny red cars look much like the originals that Andrew Hallidie designed. In fact, when you hop on, you're riding on the country's first moving National Historic Landmark.

FACT:

Three cables run San Francisco's 3 cable car lines. Each is a loop of wire rope under the street moving 9½ miles per hour. They have to be changed every few months.

There's a Cable Car Museum in the Cable Car Barn at the corner of Washington and Mason streets. This is where the cars are kept at night, and if you look over the balcony you can see the giant wheels turning, pulling the cables under San Francisco's streets. The cables are attached by a mechanical grip below each car.

When you ride the cable cars, watch the gripman. (There are no women gripmen yet, but you may meet a woman conductor.) To start the car, the gripman pulls the big lever that closes the grip around the moving cable. To stop, he steps on the wheel brakes. He has to be strong. Don't be surprised if you feel like you're riding a slow roller coaster when you're on a cable car. Look at the city as you go up and down the hills. Notice the modern skyscrapers and the colorful Victorian houses called "Painted Ladies." There are 14,000 Victorians in San Francisco and to many people, they are as much a symbol of San Francisco as are cable cars. You've probably seen them in lots of TV shows and movies.

FACT:

San Francisco is known as the City of Seven Hills, but it's really built on top of 43 hills—including one 938-feet high.

Hop off the cable car and check out Lombard Street, the most crooked street in the world. Can you imagine a horse and buggy on this squiggly cobblestone street?

Nearby, in Russian Hill, look for the narrow stairways hidden in people's gardens. This neighborhood of big old houses gets its name from Russian sailors who were buried here. You'll find some steps on Greenwich Street between

Hyde and Larkin streets. Are you ready to climb the steps up 294 feet to the top? The view is worth it.

People who think California is always sunny are in for a big surprise in San Francisco. Even in summer, don't forget your jacket. Early in the mornings and late in the afternoons, the famous San Francisco fog rolls in and blankets the city. That's why it hardly ever gets really hot here. Often it warms up during the day, but beware:

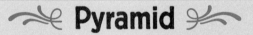

Pyramid

It looks like a tall, skinny triangle. The Transamerica Pyramid is San Francisco's tallest building—853 feet high—and the most famous.

The Pyramid is headquarters for the Transamerica Corporation, and is in the heart of downtown San Francisco. More than 1,500 people work for 50 different companies in this building.

Built in 1972, it has more than 300 miles of steel reinforcing rods. You can go up to the 27th floor to check out the view.

When the fog returns at night, it gets cold again. San Franciscans call the fog their "air conditioning."

Check out a map and you can see why San Francisco is called The City by the Bay. It's at the very tip of a peninsula, a portion of land surrounded by three bodies of water: the Pacific Ocean, the San Francisco Bay, and the famous Golden Gate—the narrow passage between them. What do you think of the orange Golden Gate Bridge? Three quarters of a million people live in San Francisco now, so you can imagine how many people cross the bridge every day.

FACT:
San Francisco was first named Yerba Buena, which means "good herb" in Spanish. The name was changed in 1847 to match the name of the bay.

Join some of San Francisco's locals playing along the water's edge, flying kites, riding bikes, and rollerblading. Did you bring a Frisbee?

It's hard to believe that San Francisco was once a sandy, tree-filled peninsula where Native Americans made their homes. Spanish explorers first stumbled on San Francisco Bay in 1769 and established a mission. Later, the Mexicans ruled the area. Then one summer day

FACT:
The Transamerica Pyramid has 3,678 windows.

in 1846, a small band of American sailors rowed ashore from their ship, raised the American flag in the small town's plaza, and claimed the land for the United States. Just 500 people lived here in 1847.

One year later, in 1848, a few sparkles found in the sand of a riverbed north of San Francisco suddenly changed everything. Soon afterward, the 1849 Gold Rush was on. Almost overnight, San Francisco became a big city overflowing with businesses and bursting with people from all over the world who were coming and

ᴥ Levi Strauss ᴥ

Twenty-five-year-old Levi Strauss came to San Francisco armed with a load of canvas fabric for making tents. But he quickly found a better use for it.

It was the middle of the Gold Rush and the miners couldn't find sturdy enough work pants. Strauss used the canvas to make the world's first jeans. They were called "waist overalls."

People couldn't get enough of "those pants of Levi's," so Strauss started peddling them in the small towns of the Gold Country.

He soon started making them out of denim. When the miners complained that their gold nuggets tore the pockets, Strauss adopted a tailor's trick of riveting the pocket corners for added strength. Today Levi Strauss & Co. still makes jeans. They're worn all over the world. You can see them being made at the San Francisco factory. But you can watch only on Wednesdays and you have to call ahead (415-565-9159).

going from the gold mines. Fortunes were made and lost, and gold seekers became known as *forty-niners*, named after the year the Gold Rush began. Now you know where San Francisco's professional football team got its name.

FACT:

San Francisco-based Levi Strauss & Co. uses close to 1.3 million miles of thread every year to make jeans—enough to wrap around the world 50 times.

San Francisco became a wild and crazy place. One neighborhood, the Barbary Coast, was notorious for its lawlessness. Right next to today's Chinatown and North Beach, the Barbary Coast was full of saloons, dance halls, gamblers, and criminals. Drunken young men were often kidnapped here and forced to work on merchant ships heading to the Far East. Sometimes they'd be gone for years.

Many newcomers to the city made their homes here. Chinese and Japanese, Hispanics, African-Americans, Italians, Irish, and Filipinos, among others, came here hoping to get rich. Many of their families have been here ever since. Notice how many different kinds of people live in San Francisco. They brought their cultures and traditions with them. That's why this is such a great place to try different kinds of food.

FACT:

It wasn't the 1906 earthquake that destroyed the city. It was the fires afterward. They burned for 3 days and nights.

Ever since the Gold Rush days, San Francisco has been known as a place where new ideas flourish and differences between people are celebrated. Artists, musicians, writers, and chefs have come here to get their start. The hippie movement began here and a lot of great rock and roll music was first played in San Francisco. Many gay Americans have migrated to the city.

However, nothing in its history has defined San Francisco's spirit more than earthquakes. Maybe you remember the earthquake that struck during the World Series at Candlestick Park in 1989. That was a strong earthquake, but the most famous is the Great San Francisco Earthquake of 1906.

Just after 5 A.M. on Wednesday, April 18, 1906, the first big shake jolted everyone out of bed. In moments, the city was changed forever.

Huge buildings collapsed. Trees uprooted. Entire houses were moved by the force of the first quake and a second one that struck that same morning. People ran around the streets in their pajamas. Thousands died. More than fifty fires blazed while huge underground water pipes broke all over town. Three-fourths of the city burned because the firefighters couldn't get water from the pipes to fight the fires.

But a few hydrants kept working. Find the gold one on Church Street near Mission Dolores. The neighbors give it a fresh coat of paint every year because, as the story goes, its water helped firefighters save the houses here.

Rebuilding started right away all across the city. San Francisco came back bigger and better than ever.

Earthquake

Millions watched the Loma Prieta earthquake on TV. It was 5:04 P.M., October 17, 1989, and people across the country were tuned in to the World Series baseball game between the San Francisco Giants and the Oakland A's at Candlestick Park. The stadium started shaking and in the end, 62 people in the Bay Area were killed and more than 3,000 were injured.

No one knows when—or where—the next major quake will strike. If you're in an earthquake, the U.S. Geological Survey suggests:

- Get under a strong piece of furniture, such as a bed.
- Don't run outdoors. Stay away from windows.
- Don't get in an elevator. Use the stairs if you have to leave a building.
- If you're in a car, pull over. Watch for falling trees and wires.

KIDS! TELL YOUR PARENTS:

Kids have less patience than adults for sight-seeing. Here's a good rule of thumb: one sight-seeing activity each day.

Make sure your parents involve you in planning the family's trip. Tell them what you want to see and do. Help them organize a schedule for each day of the trip.

The San Francisco Convention & Visitors Bureau is a good resource (415-391-2000). Call the Museum of the City of San Francisco at 415-928-0289 and the Cable Car Museum at 415-474-1887.

If you're going to be using public transportation and taking lots of cable car rides, get a MUNI Passport. It provides unlimited rides as well as some great discounts. Call 415-673-6864.

Are you a sports fan? Call the San Francisco Giants at 415-467-8000 and the Oakland Athletics at 510-638-0500. The Golden Gate Warriors play basketball at the Oakland Coliseum (510-638-6300); call the San Francisco Forty-Niners at 415-468-2249.

Here are some good books to help parents plan for their family vacation:

- *Frommer's San Francisco With Kids* ($17.00, Prentice Hall)

- *San Francisco and the Bay Area* by Barry Parr ($14.95, Compass American Guides)

- *Hidden San Francisco and Northern California* by Ray Riegert ($14.95, Ulysses Press)

FISHERMAN'S WHARF

FISHERMEN, CHOCOLATE, SHIPS, T-SHIRTS, AND PRISONERS

There are a lot more tourists than fishermen these days at Fisherman's Wharf, but the place still has the same salty seaside flavor.

Most everyone who visits San Francisco heads here first. Grab some fish and chips, or chowder served in a sourdough bread bowl, and take a good look around: You'll see boats crowded in the marinas; street performers drawing cartoons, singing, and playing instruments; a big waterfront park; ferry boats; many shops and restaurants; and of course, the sea lions who live in the water beside Pier 39.

It's a bustling place from morning until night. There's plenty to do. At Pier 39, after you've visited the sea lions (K Dock, West

⤳ Sea Lions ⤳

They dive, fight, bark, and chase sea gulls. When they get tired, they stretch out on the floating docks of the harbor to catch some sun. There are hundreds of them.

The California sea lions have made Pier 39 their home. Come watch them play. They arrived shortly after the 1989 earthquake. As soon as they discovered that there were lots of herring in the water to eat, they decided to stay and invited their friends to the never-ending party. You won't believe it until you see it.

They're huge. Male sea lions can grow to weigh 1,000 pounds and measure 7 feet long.

On weekends, look for the Marine Mammal Center volunteers. They can tell you a lot about sea lions. Do you know that some scientists think sea lions are as smart as monkeys?

Because their flippers look like fins, they're called pinnipeds, which means "fin-footed." But sea lions are mammals, like you. They've got lungs and must breathe air to live. They're warm-blooded and their babies get milk from their mothers.

Marina), go for a ride on the antique two-level Venetian carousel, or watch the mimes, jugglers, and other acts at the Crystal Geyser Center Stage. They may even ask you to join the show! If you're visiting in June, catch the Street Performers Festival. On weekends, look for Salty the Sea Lion. He roams the pier talking to visitors.

FACT:

More than 10 million people stroll Pier 39 each year. It's one of the most-visited spots in the entire country.

You can play in the arcade (the bumper cars are always fun), or shop until your parents drop. There are more than 100 stores here. You can buy everything from cable car T-shirts, kites, and chocolates to tapes, teddy bears, and posters of the Golden Gate Bridge.

FACT:

Sea lions have ear flaps and walk on all 4 flippers on land. Seals have no ear flaps and crawl on their bellies.

When you get tired of store-hopping, have a snack, take a break amid the flowers in the five-acre Waterfront Park, cruise the bay, or take a ferry to Alcatraz (ask the rangers there what programs they've got going that day).

You also might want to catch the San Francisco Experience, a multimedia show that gives you an action-packed history of the city.

Alcatraz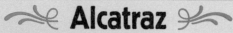

This small, rocky island is just over a mile from Fisherman's Wharf, but the prisoners sent to Alcatraz Federal Penitentiary felt as if they had been sent to the moon.

They were moved to Alcatraz because they wouldn't follow the rules at other prisons. It was a very strict place. Gangster Al Capone served time on "The Rock." So did San Francisco jewel thief Roy Gardiner and the famous Birdman of Alcatraz, Robert Stroud.

Being a prisoner here was no fun. In fact, a prisoner's worst nightmare was to be sent to Alcatraz. Take the short ferry ride over to the island and see for yourself what their days were like. Walk down "Broadway," the busiest hallway in the cellhouse, and step inside the narrow, bare cells where the prisoners lived. Look at the dark, windowless cells dubbed "The Hole," where prisoners were sent for punishment. Their meals were served through a slot in the door. Walk around their exercise yard, and imagine having to go back to a cell.

At the same time, the families of prison guards lived a normal life on the island in a regular neighborhood. Kids took the ferry to school and played outside their houses, just like you do.

Alcatraz was a federal prison for only 29 years, until 1963. Before that, the island housed a Spanish fort, then a U.S. Army fort protecting San Francisco's harbor, then a military prison. More than 100 cannons were brought here, but not one ever fired a shot to defend the bay.

Alcatraz means "pelican." You can still see pelicans on Alcatraz today.

You can see plenty of fish if you head over to Pier 45 early in the morning when the fishermen bring in their catch. If you're visiting during the first half of the year, notice the piles of Dungeness crab being sold all along the wharf. They're a San Francisco specialty.

There are non-fishy attractions along Fisherman's Wharf, too; including the Guinness Museum of World Records, Ripley's Believe It or Not Museum, and the Wax Museum.

There are also lots of old ships. Stop at the *USS Pampanito,* a World War II submarine. Imagine what it must have been like to be a sailor living for months in such cramped quarters.

You can go back in time even farther at the Hyde Street Pier. It's part of the San Francisco Maritime National Historical Park. You can board the square-rigged *Balclutha,* a ship built in the 1880s. Hundreds of ships like this one sailed from San Francisco to Europe, carrying cargo such as California wheat, and news of the Gold Rush.

FACT:

Clarence Anglin, John Anglin, and Frank Morris escaped from Alcatraz in 1962 by cutting holes in the backs of their cells. Some said they used sharpened spoons. The trio was never seen again. Many believe they drowned trying to swim away from the island.

Check out the old paddlewheel steamboat ferry *Eureka.* People rode ferries like the *Eureka* across the Bay before the Golden Gate and Bay bridges were built. This boat carried more than 2,000 passengers and 120 cars at one time!

There's also the *Thayer,* a lumber schooner that sailed from the Pacific Northwest down the California coast at the turn of the century. See if the rangers are offering any special programs on the day you visit. You might be able to learn sailors' songs, how to tie knots, or even how to catch a crab.

Not far away is the *S.S. Jeremiah O'Brien.* She's the last surviving Liberty Ship. These ships ferried troops and supplies around the world during World War II. In 1994, the *O'Brien* sailed to Europe for the 50th anniversary of D-Day. Ask your parents or grandparents about the D-Day invasion, which helped speed the end of the war.

If you like boats, you'll also want to visit the Maritime Museum. Built in the shape of a ship, it's the place to find out all about boats and San Francisco's maritime history. You'll see painted six-foot-tall figureheads and a big ship's wheel you can turn. The exhibits change regularly.

Take a breather at Aquatic Park, next to the museum. San Franciscans have come here since the 1800s to play on the sandy beach and chill out. Go for a walk along the Golden Gate Promenade. It starts here and stretches more than three miles to Fort Point. Do you have a kite? This is a good place for you to fly one.

FACT: The secret to sourdough bread is saving a bit of batter for the next loaf. The "mother dough" used today by the Boudin Sourdough Bakery, the original maker of sourdough bread, dates from 1849.

FACT: Each year, about 20 million pounds of freshly caught fish—cod, crab, swordfish, sole, salmon, and herring—is brought into the ports around San Francisco Bay.

Don't worry if you still haven't found that perfect souvenir. There are plenty of shops to explore. Stop at the Cannery. It's an old Del Monte food-packing plant that now houses a mini-mall. And of course there's Ghirardelli Square, San Francisco's most famous mall. It's built in the old Ghirardelli Chocolate Co. factory. Look for the big GHIRARDELLI sign on the roof. Hungry again? Have a sundae while you watch Ghirardelli chocolate being made in giant vats. It smells great and the sundaes are huge!

FACT:

In a year, the Ghirardelli chocolate factory produces enough chocolate chips to stack from here to the moon.

⇜ Ghirardelli ⇝

Just like everyone else rushing to San Francisco during the Gold Rush, 32-year-old Domingo Ghirardelli was looking for gold. He didn't have much luck.

But the Italian immigrant was a skilled candymaker and a smart man. He started whipping up chocolate and other treats to sell to the miners. By 1851, business was so good that Ghirardelli built a big factory in San Francisco where Ghirardelli Square is today.

You can still buy Ghirardelli chocolate bars at Ghirardelli Square and just about everywhere else in San Francisco. But now it's all made across the bay in the town of San Leandro: 40,000 pounds a year.

KIDS! TELL YOUR PARENTS:

Souvenirs are expensive. That's why it's a good idea to decide how much money everyone in the family can spend before you start shopping on Fisherman's Wharf. Talk about how much your parents will give you. Then decide how much you can bring from your savings, if you have some. What kind of souvenir do you want? A T-shirt? An Alcatraz coin? A poster or postcard?

Not everyone likes to shop. Ask your family to limit shopping to a certain amount of time, so you don't spend all day wandering in and out of stores.

If you're planning to visit Alcatraz, consider buying ferry tickets ahead of time to avoid being disappointed. For information call the **Red & White Fleet** at **800-229-2784.** For tickets call **415-546-2700.** (The fleet also operates bay cruises and ferries from Fisherman's Wharf to Tiburon, Sausalito, Angel Island, and Vallejo—where Marine World Africa USA is located.)

Pier 39 offers a free marine activity book called *Salty, the Sea and You.* To order, call 415-705-5500 or write Pier 39, P.O. Box 193730, San Francisco, CA 94119-3730.

Call the San Francisco Maritime National Historical Park at 415-556-3002.

Nearby Fort Mason houses the headquarters of the Golden Gate National Recreation Area as well as the offices of many local arts groups, theaters, and museums, including the Mexican Museum. It exhibits Mexican and Latino art, and one Sunday a month is devoted to family activities. Call 415-441-0445. All kinds of other activities are staged outside Fort Mason. It's also a good place to picnic. Call 415-441-5705.

Kids! _Use this page for your stories and drawings!_

CHINATOWN, NORTH BEACH, AND JAPANTOWN

FORTUNE COOKIES, SPAGHETTI, AND CHERRY BLOSSOMS

Walk through the Chinatown Gate on Grant Avenue at Bush Street and you'll feel like you're in a different country. Notice the street signs in both Chinese and English—you've just entered Chinatown. Look at the brightly painted, pagoda-style buildings and red and gold street lights, the

Chinese newspapers and magazines, and the foods in the store windows. You'll notice all kinds of things in the shops that you've probably never seen before: fancy jade jewelry; Oriental dresses and furniture; whole roasted ducks and pigs; piles of shark fins and sea slugs; and big vats of *jook,* the creamy rice dish the Chinese like to eat for breakfast. How about some 1,000-year-old eggs? They've actually only been preserved for a few months, but they look ancient because they've turned brown outside. If you cracked one, you'd see that the yolk is green.

FACT:

Shark's fin is an expensive Chinese delicacy that sells for more than $100 a pound and is used in soup. The golden fin represents prosperity.

The 24 blocks of Chinatown are narrow, crooked, and crowded. Thousands of Chinese immigrants and Chinese-Americans live here, making Chinatown one of the most crowded neighborhoods in the country. Many residents don't speak English, and some of the older people never venture outside Chinatown. Why should they? It has everything they need—banks, stores, clubs, churches, playgrounds, and jobs.

Start at Portsmouth Square. Some people call this Chinatown's living room. You'll see lots of seniors playing poker and Chinese

FACT:

Most of the workers who built the Central Pacific Railroad, which connected California to the rest of the U.S., were Chinese.

chess. They come here every day. Grandmothers visit with one another as they watch their grandchildren play.

Portsmouth Square is where San Francisco really began. A whaling ship captain named William Richardson pitched a tent, then built San Francisco's first house here in 1835.

Ten years after that, Chinese workers started coming to San Francisco by the thousands. At first, like everyone else, they came to look for gold. (In China, San Francisco became known as *Gum San Dai Fow,* "Big City of the Gold Mountain.")

FACT:

Kites were invented thousands of years ago in China.

Later, they came for jobs. San Francisco's rapidly growing population needed all sorts of services, so there was plenty for hard-working immigrants to do. The Chinese ran laundries, opened clothing factories and restaurants, worked on the railroad that would connect the city to the rest of the country, and built Chinatown. But from the beginning, Chinese men—women didn't come until later—were treated cruelly. A lot of miners resented the

Chinese. Discriminatory laws were passed against them. It was hard for them to buy property.

Much of Chinatown was destroyed in the 1906 earthquake, and there was talk of moving the neighborhood elsewhere. But it was rebuilt here, complete with the Chinese-style buildings you see today.

To learn more about Chinatown history, visit the Chinese

Dim Sum

In Chinese, dim sum means "point to the heart." Instead of ordering from a menu, servers wheel the food around on carts. You point to what you want from the assortment of dishes, such as dumplings stuffed with a variety of fillings: shrimp and pork, vegetables, and beef. Act fast before the waiter or waitress whizzes by.

People in San Francisco eat dim sum for lunch or brunch. It's delicious!

Here's a guide to help you choose, courtesy of Chinatown expert Shirley Fong-Torres:

- *Cha Sil Bow*—steamed pork bun
- *Chern Goon*—egg rolls
- *Jin Dooey*—sesame-seed ball filled with lotus paste
- *No Mi Gai*—lotus leaf stuffed with sticky rice, chicken, pork, and shrimp
- *Lo Bok Go*—turnip cake
- *Gee Bow Gai*—paper-wrapped chicken

FACT:

Fortune cookies were invented in San Francisco, but not in Chinatown. They were served first at the Japanese Tea Garden in Golden Gate Park. Chinese restaurants borrowed the idea. Now they're served in Chinese restaurants everywhere and are exported all over the world, even to China.

Historical Society of America on Commercial Street.

People come from all over the world to shop and eat in Chinatown. You'll see small, busy restaurants everywhere, upstairs and downstairs. Many of the customers are eating with chopsticks. Try them out on some Chinese noodle dishes.

Another thing to try is tea from a Chinese tea shop. There are hundreds of teas to choose from. The Chinese drink tea at all times of the day. Sharing a cup of tea is a sign of respect and friendship. For thousands of years, different herbal teas have been used as medicines. If you're lucky, you might see a tea ceremony. Notice the tiny cups and pot. The small size speeds the brewing process.

Stop in at an herbalist's shop. The Chinese come here to get ingredients for herbal teas and soups that they believe will help keep them healthy. Some of the remedies have been used for centuries. Try some Tiger Balm for sore muscles, or deer antler (usually ground up and added to soup) for strength. Bird's nest soup is thought to be good for your skin.

For a sweeter taste sensation, duck into Ross Alley and visit the

❧ Angel Island ❧

Angel Island is a big nature preserve in the middle of San Francisco Bay. Local families come to this state park to picnic, bike, and hike.

But there's a lot of history on Angel Island, too. Visit the old Civil War camp and Army fort.

Between 1910 and 1940, immigrants from Asia came through Angel Island. Many Chinese people were held here, often for months, as they tried to prove their family connection to those who were already here. Those without fathers or husbands in the United States commonly became "paper sons and daughters" and "paper brides" to sponsors in the Chinese-American community. Documents such as birth certificates were forged and sold.

Many Chinese-American families got their start with a "paper" son or daughter.

tiny Golden Gate Fortune Cookie Factory. Watch the women grab the hot, flat cookies off the press and quickly fold them, tucking the fortunes inside. Each worker makes 1,200 cookies an hour!

Walk just a few blocks north and you'll enter pizza and spaghetti land. Welcome to North Beach, the home of many generations of Italian-Americans. Pick your favorite pizza. They're sure to have it.

Italian fisherman and laborers settled here before the 1906 earthquake, and the neighborhood has had a strong Italian flavor ever since. This is the place to eat pasta in San Francisco and there are dozens of restaurants to choose from. At The Stinking Rose, garlic is the specialty. Have you ever had garlic ice cream? You can try it here.

In the 1950s, North Beach was famous for the poets and artists who came here from all over the county. They were called "beatniks" and were known for wearing black turtleneck shirts and putting poetry to music. You'll still see artists,

FACT:

North Beach is not a beach but a famous San Francisco neighborhood settled by Italian fishermen and laborers in the early years of this century. Later it became home to writers and artists. There are more than 75 Italian restaurants within a few blocks of this neighborhood.

poets, and musicians gathering in the coffeehouses here, writing, and sketching in books.

Look for the green and yellow wild parrots who fly around the neighborhood, from Washington Square to Coit Tower to crooked

Lillie Hitchcock Coit

One day on her way home from school, Lillie Coit helped San Francisco firefighters douse a blaze. She became their lifelong friend, smoking cigars and playing poker with the firemen, even wearing an honorary firefighter's uniform. This was in the days long before any women were firefighters, even before most women wore pants.

Throughout Coit's life, it was said that she would drop anything to chase a fire engine. Though she left San Francisco and lived abroad for much of her life, she never forgot her firefighter friends and she returned to the city shortly before her death in 1929. She left money in her will to help make San Francisco more beautiful. The 180-foot Coit Tower was built on top of Telegraph Hill in 1933. She also donated a famous statue in Washington Square of two firefighters rescuing a young girl.

Lombard Street. They chatter loudly, so you may hear them before you see them.

Stop by Washington Square around 8 A.M. and you'll see nearly 100 people practicing Tai Chi, an ancient Chinese exercise. They look like they're moving in slow motion, but they're using every muscle in their bodies.

Not enough exercise for you? Then head up Telegraph Hill to Coit Tower. Here you'll have one of the best views of the city.

A few miles away, in Japantown, you'll find a very different type of monument—the 100-foot-high Peace Pagoda. Head west to this neighborhood for an introduction to another of San Francisco's many cultures.

FACT:

The Japanese have celebrated the arrival of the cherry blossoms every spring for more than 1,000 years.

The Japanese have lived here since after the Great Earthquake of 1906. During World War II, when the United States was at war with Japan, Japanese-American citizens were forced to leave their homes and live in camps. It was a terrible time. But after the war, many returned, and today at least 12,000 Japanese-Americans live in San Francisco.

Walk around the shops in the Japan Center. Thousands of people come here every spring for the Cherry Blossom Festival. Try some sushi. Sound weird? Ask some Japanese-American kids about it. They'll tell you raw fish can be pretty tasty.

KIDS! TELL YOUR PARENTS:

San Francisco is famous all over the world for great food and restaurants. In addition to Chinese, Italian, and Japanese, there's Mexican, Thai, Korean, French, Vietnamese, and lots of other foods you've never tasted before.

But you shouldn't be forced to eat anything. That's no fun. The last thing you want on vacation is to fight about food. If you don't want to risk ordering something you've never seen before for dinner, ask your parents to order a dish everyone can try. Or sample something as a snack rather than as an entire meal.

Chinatown is a great place to do that. A wonderful way to see Chinatown is to take a walking tour that ends with a dim sum lunch. Try Wok Wiz at 415-355-9657 or Chinatown Discovery Tours at 415-982-8839. Another good bet is to use the guidebook *San Francisco Chinatown: A Walking Tour with Shirley Fong-Torres* (China Books, $10.95).

To find out more about North Beach, call the North Beach Chamber of Commerce at 415-403-0666. For information on Japantown's Cherry Blossom Festival, call 415-563-2313.

Kids! Use this page for your stories and drawings!

GOLDEN GATE PARK

Bison, Tea, Skateboards, and Waves

Grab a skateboard. Hop on a bike. Strap on those blades. Take a kite and a baseball mitt and head for Golden Gate Park.

There's so much to do here you won't want to leave.

Golden Gate is one huge park: It contains 1,017 acres of trees,

FACT:

While San Francisco was being rebuilt after the 1906 earthquake, children attended tent schools and tended garden plots in Golden Gate Park. Tens of thousands of people left homeless by the quake camped in tents all over the park.

grass, hiking paths, bike trails, baseball diamonds, basketball courts, a golf course, tennis courts, playgrounds, ponds, museums, and outdoor concert spaces. You'll even find a herd of grazing bison, and a Dutch windmill in the middle of a tulip garden.

Take along a fishing pole and you can practice casting in front of Angler's Lodge.

Rent a horse at Golden Gate Stables or take a riding lesson. The park has 12 miles of bridle paths.

If cycling or skating is more your speed, you can rent a bike or skates at many spots near the park. You can go for miles in Golden Gate Park. Stop and pitch some horseshoes. Eat a picnic lunch. Visit the Touch Pool at the Steinhart Aquarium and feel a starfish.

Sail a model boat on Spreckels Lake (bring your own). It's fun to watch people sail their

FACT:

Portions of Golden Gate Park are closed to traffic on Sundays. During that time, you'll find lots of people and their pets playing in the streets.

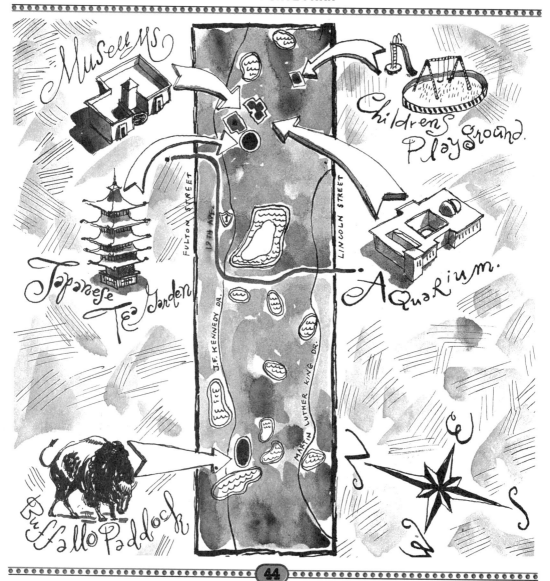

FACT:

Bison have lived in Golden Gate Park for nearly 100 years. The current herd was brought from Wyoming in 1984.

models on weekends. While you're there, walk over to the Buffalo Paddock to see the bison. Or rent a rowboat at Stow Lake.

On Sundays, you might be able to hear the Golden Gate Park Band play. The concerts are free.

You won't want to skip the huge Children's Playground. The slides are plenty steep and glide right over some rocks. You'll want to go down again and again. There's a huge climbing structure, plus gymnastics equipment, and lots of sand for digging. The old carousel with its painted horses, pigs, and cats is right next door. Kids ride for a quarter. (It's free if you're less than 39 inches tall.)

It's hard to imagine that this whole place was once a huge sand dune. It was called the Great Sand Wastes, and many believed a park could never be built here. They couldn't have been more wrong.

FACT:

Golden Gate Park is home to the oldest park playground in the country. Kids still love the Mary B. Connolly Children's Playground. It was built in 1888.

Stop and look at all the pretty flowers, different ones for different seasons—roses and dahlias, cherry blossoms and magnolias, and tulips. You'll also see a redwood grove and a garden planted with all the plants mentioned in Shakespeare's plays. Stroll through the Botanical Gardens (check out the dwarf

Surf and Sand Castles

People have come to the Cliff House at Ocean Beach for more than 100 years. Thousands used to swim in the huge Sutro Baths. There were 6 swimming pools under a glass ceiling. The pools held 1,685 gallons of sea water, and they were filled and emptied by the tides.

The pools are gone now and the sea lions who used to play on Seal Rocks have moved to Pier 39, but it's still fun to climb around the ruins of Sutro Baths. You'll see plenty of exotic birds that you probably won't see at home. Head up to the Cliff House, where you can eat a sandwich while you watch the ocean waves crash.

Take some quarters and head downstairs in the Cliff House to the Musée Mecanique. There's an entire collection of old-fashioned mechanical games and devices here that kids used to play at arcades before video games were invented. They're still fun. Make the old firemen race up the ladders, or the farm animals eat.

From the Cliff House, you can hike down to Ocean Beach and walk for miles along the Pacific coast. Head south to Fort Funston where you might see hang gliders. If you go north, you can build sand forts at China Beach and Baker Beach. You probably won't want to swim, though. The water is usually cold and the waves are fierce.

plants), or the Conservatory of Flowers. This mostly glass building was shipped in pieces from England. It's the oldest building in the park, finished in 1879.

Everyone loves the Japanese Tea Garden. Built entirely by Japanese artisans, the Tea Garden celebrated its 100th birthday in 1994. Many of the buildings here were built for the 1894 California International Exposition.

The Japanese Tea Garden's claim to fame is that the fortune cookie was invented here. Today, you can have Japanese tea and cookies in the tea house. Climb over the Drum Bridge. It looks like a semicircle and is as steep as a ladder. Look at the giant statue of Buddha. He's called

FACT:

The Japanese consider a garden to be a work of art. Plants and stones are arranged in a specific way to harmonize with nature.

The Buddha Who Sits Through Sun and Rain Without Shelter.

Also make sure you see the giant carp swimming in the pond.

Don't worry if it starts raining. Just head over to the California Academy of Sciences and take your pick of indoor activities. Go on a 3.5-billion-year trip through time, meeting some life-size dinosaurs along the way. Feel an earthquake at the Safequake exhibit. Visit the hands-on Discovery Room and try on clothes from other countries. Look at the stars in the Morrison Planetarium (some evenings you can see the Laserium show, too).

❦ The Haight ❦

Teenagers filled this neighborhood wearing bell-bottom pants, tie-dyed shirts, and love beads. Everyone had long hair. Candles and incense and music were everywhere. Many rock groups, including The Grateful Dead, got their start here, as did the first free medical clinic in the country.

By the summer of 1967, tens of thousands of "flower children" from around the world had made their way to the Haight, a neighborhood just east of Golden Gate Park.

Today, Haight Street still attracts youth pop culture. The hippie scene has been replaced by the "grunge" scene and the area has become more commercial. Visitors from all over the world, however, still come here to discover new music and fashions and people-watch from cafe windows.

You also can see more than 1,000 different rocks at Gem and Mineral Hall; watch thousands of different fish at the Steinhart Aquarium, some of which will surround you in the Fish Roundabout; stop at the alligator swamp; and say "hi" to the penguins.

If you like art, Golden Gate Park has something for you, too. The M.H. de Young Memorial Museum and the Asian Art Museum are both just across the road from the Academy of Sciences. Ask about special kids' programs. Look at the American and British paintings at the de Young Museum; the Asian museum is the

∽≪ The Zoo ≫∼

Polar bears look white but their skin is actually black. The bears seem white because light bounces off of their fur, which is clear, not white at all.

You can see polar bears and hundreds of other animals—koalas, penguins, gorillas, rhinos, lions, and tigers—at the San Francisco Zoological Gardens and Children's Zoo. It's one of the best zoos in the country and is known for its efforts to breed endangered animals, such as the California condor. Stop at the Primate Discovery Center to see many kinds of endangered monkeys.

Visit Penguin Island and the five-acre Children's Zoo. Feed the goats and watch the zookeepers tend to some of the baby animals.

Don't miss Gorilla World. It's one of the planet's biggest gorilla exhibits, with plenty of space for you to watch the gentle giants play. See what a good job Bawang does caring for her baby son?

largest collection of its kind outside Asia. The exhibits cover 6,000 years of art history.

Don't forget to wear your tennis shoes—your feet will get a real workout exploring Golden Gate Park.

KIDS! TELL YOUR PARENTS:

No matter how many interesting places there are to see on vacation, you'll still want to spend lots of time playing outside. After all, vacations are for fun. For every indoor activity, plan some outdoor time at playgrounds, beaches, or parks. Everyone will be happier, and San Francisco has plenty of options.

For information about the Academy of Sciences, call 415-750-7145. Call 415-750-7141 for Planetarium information and 415-750-7138 for Laserium show times. To ask about family-friendly programs at the M.H. de Young Memorial Museum, call 415-863-3330.

For Asian Art Museum information call 415-668-8921. (The California Palace of the Legion of Honor, located north of the park, is closed for renovations until 1995.)

If you're planning to visit the museums, the Conservatory of Flowers, and the Japanese Tea Garden, in Golden Gate Park, a Golden Gate Culture Pass offers savings on admission to all five of the attractions. Call the San Francisco Visitor Information Center at 415-391-2000.

Even better, if you're visiting on the first Wednesday or Thursday of the month, admission to many San Francisco museums is free.

GOLDEN GATE BRIDGE AND THE EXPLORATORIUM

KID-SIZE SCIENCE, CANNONS, AND MODEL Ts

Take a walk across the Golden Gate Bridge. Now you can really see how big it is. The main portion stretches 4,200 feet over the water. The towers are as tall as a skyscraper, rising 746 feet above sea level.

Nothing says "San Francisco" to the world more than the

Golden Gate Bridge. It's hard to believe that a lot of people didn't want the bridge built. They thought it would ruin the landscape.

Bridge builder Joseph Strauss worked for 13 years promoting his idea. Finally, San Franciscans voted to give the bridge a try. It took four years and $35 million to build. The Golden Gate Bridge opened May 27, 1937. More than 200,000 people walked across it that day.

On your way to the bridge, stop at Fort Point just beneath the south tower of the bridge, near the water's edge. It's a great place to get a close-up view of the bridge and to find out more about the

FACT:

Fort Point's walls are so thick they could have withstood 10,000 cannonballs, but the fort was never attacked.

❧ Bridge Builders ❧

No one got rich building the Golden Gate Bridge. Many of the bridge builders worked for less than $1 a day. They worked so high up it took them more than half an hour to climb to their jobs. But they were glad for the work. It was the middle of the Great Depression and jobs were hard to get.

Building the bridge was dangerous work. A huge trapeze-style net hung 60 feet below the men to catch them if they fell, but it didn't always work. Eleven men died building the bridge. The net saved 19 others from the icy water below. These survivors called themselves the Halfway to Hell Club.

soldiers who were stationed here during the Civil War. You might even be able to help load a cannon.

For another kind of adventure, visit the nearby Exploratorium, where you'll find some of the coolest science experiments. Many people think this is the best science museum in the country. The Exploratorium is designed for kids. There are more than 650 different spots where you can make something happen. You'll pick up some fun facts about electricity, gravity, colors, and hearing, plus many other parts of our world.

The Exploratorium's home is in the Palace of Fine Arts. The outside is decorated with domes that look like Greek Temples. Inside, it's every kid's idea of what a science class should be. There are no walls here—just a gigantic two-acre space filled with all kinds of amazing things.

Everywhere you look, there are cranks to turn,

FACT:

The Golden Gate Bridge is orange, not gold. It got its name from the channel that's underneath: The mile-wide Golden Gate Channel is the entrance to San Francisco Bay from the Pacific Ocean.

FACT:

More than 5,000 gallons of paint are used on the Golden Gate Bridge every year. A part of it always is being painted. The orange color was chosen because it complements the skyline.

buttons to push, sounds to hear, knobs to pull, and computers to operate. Each exhibit is designed to let you learn something about science by performing experiments yourself. Your parents will have as much fun as you do moving from station to station humming into an echo tube,

EXPLORATORIUM

finger painting on a computer, and watching screens of ocean waves.

FACT:

Your eye is a light trap: Light enters through the pupil and bounces around. Very little bounces out, which is why your pupil looks black.

Step into the Shadow Box, where a phosphorescent material lets you leave your shadow—in midair! Design a giant bubble with yourself inside. Head over to the Tornado and stand inside as a column of mist swirls into a tunnel. Go into the Distorted Room and watch yourself shrink and grow. Help dissect a cow's eye.

Record yourself on a video camera, then create a colorful kaleidoscope of your movements.

If you're 7 or older, you won't want to miss the Tactile Dome. (Tell your parents they have to make reservations for it ahead of time.) Take off your shoes and socks and crawl through a pitch-black space. Feel your way as you slide, climb, and grope to the end, straight into a vat of dried beans. Each time you make your way through—you'll have many chances in your allotted hour—you'll feel different things. Did you notice the oddly shaped globs? It's a trip you won't forget.

Take a break at Crissy Field. This is a great place to run—just ask the joggers. On a windy day, you might see some windsurfers on the water, and some baseball players on land. Did you bring

❧ Make A Circus ❧

Make sure to visit parks during the summer. That's where the Make*A*Circus troupe performs its magic. Kids can be part of the action, and it's all free.

First, there's a regular circus, complete with acrobats, jugglers, and clowns. Next, kids from the audience can learn to do some of the circus skills they've just watched. Finally, the kids make a circus themselves, performing for the audience. Call 415-776-8470 to find out where you can help Make*A*Circus.

your mitt and ball?

Stop a few blocks away on Lombard Street at Mel's Drive-In for a great burger and fries. Play some of the oldies on the juke box.

If you're driving across the Golden Gate Bridge, head for some more hands-on fun at the Bay Area Discovery Museum in Sausalito. It's housed in 7 old buildings at Fort Baker, and it's jammed full of indoor and outdoor activities for kids.

See if you can get through the Maze of Illusions. Did you see the holograph? Make your own video in the Media Center, or build a sculpture out of clay in the Art Center. Pump "gas" into the Model T (it's a real one!) outside in the old-fashioned gas station, or play in the ArtPark next door. Put on a hard hat and build a skyscraper out of plastic bricks in the Architecture Building, or "fish" from a

Discovery Boat in the San Francisco Bay Hall. If there weren't so much fun in store for you other places, you wouldn't want to leave.

KIDS! TELL YOUR PARENTS:

Don't try to see everything in a museum—even a museum aimed at kids—in just one visit. It's much better to concentrate on the exhibits that interest all of you. Stop and discuss what you're seeing. Does everyone understand the concept? What's neat about it? Quit when everyone is tired and hungry.

Before you go, plan your visit together. Is there a special exhibit you don't want to miss? Are there other things you could skip? Keep in mind that the Exploratorium is geared to school-age kids, although there always are plenty of younger children around. At a science museum as big as the Exploratorium, or at a major art museum, it might be wise to take a break outside for awhile, then head back for more. The Bay Area Discovery Museum has a park right on the grounds.

To make reservations for the Tactile Dome at the Exploratorium, call 415-561-0362 several weeks ahead. For general museum information, call 415-561-0360. Admission to the Exploratorium is free the first Wednesday of the month.

Call the Bay Area Discovery Museum at 415-332-7674. Ask about special programs and activities.

To find out when the cannon drills at Fort Point are scheduled, call 415-556-1693.

Kids! Use this page for your stories and drawings!

MARIN COUNTY

BABY SEALS, REDWOOD TRAILS, AND WHALES

Each patient gets lots of tender loving care, as well as checkups and medicines. But they get their pills served up inside raw fish. And these patients may weigh hundreds of pounds. Welcome to the Marine Mammal Center, a very special hospital where sick seals and sea lions, as well as whales,

FACT:

Harbor seal pups can swim at birth but are almost always born on land. Mothers frequently leave them on the beach while they look for food. If you see a seal pup, don't touch it or get too close. It can be difficult to reunited a mother and a pup if the pup's been moved.

dolphins, and porpoises, are cared for. It's up on a hill in the Marin Headlands, just north of the Golden Gate Bridge. You can visit any day of the year.

Scientists and hundreds of volunteers work together to take care of wild marine creatures who are sick or injured. They bring the animals here from along the Northern California coast after people call and report seeing an animal in need of help. The patients may have been bitten by sharks, or cut on boat propellers, or have a disease

∼❦ Sausalito and Tiburon ❦∼

Both are tiny towns known for their cute houses, restaurants, and shops. Come over for breakfast by the water's edge. If you like to shop with your family, there are plenty of places to browse. Check out all the fancy yachts in Sausalito. Stop at the San Francisco Bay Model to see a model of the bay, complete with tides coming in and out. (Call 415-332-3870 to see when the model is being demonstrated.) Tiburon's Blackie's Pasture is a good kite-flying spot. Another fun thing to do is to watch birds at the National Audubon Society's Richardson Bay Wildlife Sanctuary.

that's made them weak. Some might be sick from eating garbage. They may stay for months before they're well enough to return to the wild.

FACT:

Sea lions can dive as deep as 800 feet and swim as fast as 25 miles an hour.

There are new patients all the time. Most survive. Some are huge, some are just babies. The center's staff takes care of them 24 hours a day, just the way doctors and nurses would take care of you in the hospital. If not for the staff and volunteers, many of these animals wouldn't make it on their own in the ocean.

❧ John Muir ☙

John Muir loved the woods. Born in Scotland and raised in Wisconsin, he traveled the country, walking 1,000 miles from Indianapolis to the Georgia coast to the Gulf of Mexico. He eventually sailed to Cuba, then to California.

He first visited the Yosemite Valley in 1868, before it became a park. He returned the next year to work as a shepherd. He built a cabin and roamed the park, learning all he could.

Muir began to speak out about the need to conserve the land and save the animals. Gradually, people began to listen—including President Theodore Roosevelt.

Muir's efforts led to Yosemite becoming a national park in 1890. Two years later, he became the founder and first president of the Sierra Club.

In the Bay Area, he's considered a great protector of nature, and that's why Muir Woods is named after him.

If you love the great outdoors, you couldn't be in a better spot than here. Golden Gate National Recreation Area offers plenty of rolling hills and wildflowers, coves, beaches, and rocky cliffs.

One of the most famous parts of this area is Muir Woods, a place to see some amazing giant trees. This grove of towering redwoods is all that's left of the redwood forests that once surrounded San Francisco Bay. The tallest tree here is 253 feet high.

Stop at the Visitor's Center and get a free Discovery Pack. They're made especially for kids and contain things like binoculars, magnifying lenses, and bug boxes. Look for woodpecker holes in the trees. Do you know that trees help rid

FACT:

The oldest coast redwoods in Muir Woods are more than 1,000 years old. They have special bark that is up to a foot thick and very fire-resistant. A chemical inside called *tannin* gives the trees their red color and helps keep them safe from insects and bacteria.

FACT:

Ladybugs live for a year. They are carried by the wind to Muir Woods where they clump together in big groups. Ladybugs' color and their horrible taste as well as their smell—to animals, not people—is enough to keep their enemies away.

the air of pollutants?

Look at rings in the cross-sectioned tree on display and in the fallen trees along the path. A tree grows one ring each year. Count the rings and you can tell how old these trees are. Some of these trees were already 500 years old when Columbus landed in America.

The best time to see animals is early in the morning or late in the afternoon. On nice days in the fall and winter, you might see some monarch butterflies. In the summer, look for lady bugs. There are blacktail deer, chipmunks, ravens, snakes, lizards, wrens, and bright blue Steller's jays. Northern spotted owls live here, too, but aren't easily seen.

Look for the big hollows in some of the trees. Pioneers called them "goosepens." In some redwoods the space is so big that pioneers kept cattle, sheep, chickens, and geese in them.

Stay on the flat, paved trails and explore the

FACT:

Baby gray whales are 12 to 15 feet long and weigh about 1,500 pounds.

edge of the creek. Or, for a bigger challenge, hike a little more than 3 miles to Mount Tamalpais State Park. Local kids like to hike up "Mount Tam" and camp in the park. There's good mountain biking, too. In the spring, look for waterfalls.

If you feel like hitting the sand, hike from Muir Woods 3 miles to Muir Beach, or farther to Stinson Beach. Don't forget your water bottle.

FACT:

Millions of years ago, whales' ancestors lived on land and walked on feet. They come from the same family as wolves and horses.

~~ Gray Whales ~~

Look for the "blow." When a whale comes up to breathe, it spews a cloud of air and water as high as 15 feet. Watch for blows 30 to 50 seconds apart.

Each winter, thousands of gray whales travel south from Alaska along California's coast to Baja, where they have their babies in the warmer water before continuing farther south. The 5,000-mile trip is the longest distance any mammal migrates. The whales travel in small groups, staying fairly close to the shoreline. Each day they cover 70 to 80 miles, surfacing every few minutes to breathe. In the spring, they return with their new babies.

It's not easy to spot the whales from the shore, but many people like to try. A better way is to go out on a whale-watching boat. Many trips are offered along the California coast. If you're lucky, you'll see the whales jump out of the water and fall back, making a huge splash. That's called "breaching." Don't forget your binoculars.

In the winter, Muir Beach Overlook is a good spot to whale watch. Local kids love the miles of sand at Stinson Beach.

Not far from here is Bolinas Lagoon Preserve, where you might get a good look at great blue herons and egrets in their tree-top homes at the Audubon Canyon Ranch. It's open only on weekends and some holidays in summer.

Head farther north to the spectacular wild, rocky beaches of Point Reyes National Seashore. Ask about special kids' programs at the Bear Valley Visitor Center. You can tour a replica of a Miwok

FACT:

An earthquake's *epicenter* is the point on the ground where the greatest movement occurs. A *seismograph* is the instrument that records earth tremors and shows an earthquake's size.

Indian village; take a walk along the San Andreas Fault—where the 1906 earthquake started; meet the horses at the Morgan Horse Ranch; or build gigantic sand castles on the beach.

Bring a sweatshirt. It's going to be windy, but perfect for beach-

✦ San Andreas Fault ✦

When you walk along the San Andreas fault the land to your left is moving in a different direction than the land to your right. Its movement helps to shape the surface of the earth. The *fault* is the boundary between the North American and Pacific parts of the earth's surface, called "plates." Geologists think the outer layer of the Earth is divided into about a dozen large plates and many smaller ones that float on a softer layer underneath.

Powerful forces driven by heat deep in the Earth's mantle make the plates move. They may collide, separate, or slide right past each other. Along the San Andreas Fault, the Pacific plate slowly is moving to the northwest about 2 inches a year. Most of the time, we don't even notice. But on April 18, 1906, the Point Reyes peninsula suddenly jumped 20 feet. That caused the devastating San Francisco earthquake. Point Reyes' Earthquake Trail (just outside the Bear Valley Visitor Center) shows you where this happened. Can you find where (legend has it) the cow fell into the gap?

combing at the great beach. You can sunbathe at Drake's Beach, explore tide pools, look for harbor seals, or whale watch outside the Point Reyes Lighthouse—famous because so many ships crashed along the rocky coast here before it was built. Remember to smear on the sunscreen.

KIDS! TELL YOUR PARENTS:

The best way to learn about nature is to slow down and take your time. Don't rush it! Stop at the visitors center to gather information. Take time to participate in special programs for kids or families. You'll get a lot more out of your visits to the parks that way.

Your parents will probably get just as involved as you do looking for animals, measuring tree rings, and hiking. Nature is one thing everyone can enjoy together.

For information about the Marine Mammal Center, call 415-289-SEAL. (The Mammal Center also sponsors some programs at Pier 39. Visit the Interpretive Center there to find out about them.)

Call Muir Woods at 415-388-2595. Call Mount Tamalpais State Park at 415-388-2070, and the Marin Headlands Visitor Center for information and campground reservations at 415-331-1540. Call Muir Beach at 415-388-2596, and Stinson Beach at 415-868-1922. The Bolinas Lagoon Preserve can be reached at 415-868-9244.

For Point Reyes National Seashore information, call 415-663-1092.

Kids! *Use this page for your stories and drawings!*

SAN JOSE, BERKELEY, AND NAPA
GEYSERS, GRAPES, COLLEGE, AND MYSTERIES

I f you think museums are boring, you haven't been to the Children's Discovery Museum of San Jose. Look for the big purple building in Guadalupe River Park.

Go ahead. Turn a few cartwheels in the middle of the museum. There's enough room. Make noise. Touch anything you

Computer Chip

Regular Size Pencil

want. No one will stop you.

This place is huge—one of the biggest children's museums in the country. The idea is for you to explore the connections between yourself and the world around you while you play.

There's a replica of a city street that lets you slide "underground" to see what a sewer looks like. Other activities help you imagine life in the old days. Have you ever tried washing clothes with a washing board?

You can grind and press corn tortillas (eat them, too!), make jewelry in the Doodad Dump, pump Waterworks' pedals that move water from one level to another, and even crack a safe at the Kid's Bank. Play at the Early Childhood Resource Center. Then check out your heart rate in the Kid's Care Clinic. Meet Seemore Boneapart, the museum's resident skeleton.

Want to know another special thing about San Jose? You're surrounded by more people who know more about computers than in any other place in the world. San Jose was the first capital of California. Today it's the worldwide capital of the computer industry. It's the perfect place to see how technology has changed our lives.

That's exactly what the Tech Museum of Innovation does. Walk over from the children's museum and watch a 9-foot-square microchip light up as it answers your questions. Do you know that a real microchip would fit on your fingertip?

Watch a robot draw your portrait. Design a bicycle on a computer. Look at the 23-foot-high double helix made of 500 phone books. The double helix is the shape of DNA, and one tiny DNA molecule contains as much information as those phone books.

Before you leave, stop in the Clean Room—not for a shower, but to see how microchips are made.

FACT:

"Silicon Valley" is the nickname given to the area of Northern California where the computer industry got its start. The computer world is centered in the San Jose area, with more than 3,000 high-tech companies located there. The tiny chips that control computers are made from silicon, which is how the valley got its name.

If you want to see how the most complex computer—your brain—works, head north from San Jose to Berkeley and the Lawrence Hall of Science, high on a hill on the University of California, Berkeley campus. This is another place that will show you how science can be a lot of fun. Do you know that you need to keep "exercising" your brain by using it?

See if you can find your way out of a giant maze. Stop a laser beam bare-handed. Climb all over the life-size whale and 5-foot-high, 60-foot-long DNA molecule outside. Visit the Holt Planetarium.

Great America

Calling all roller coaster maniacs—Paramount's Great America has got your number.

The Grizzly has the tallest wooden coaster lift in Northern California. Top Gun™ features a 100-foot lift and a 360-degree turn. Ride the Vortex stand-up coaster through all kinds of steel loops and twists. Make two 360-degree loops on the Demon. And then there are water coasters, such as Whitewater Falls and Rip Roaring Rapids.

There are 30 rides in all at the 100-acre amusement park in Santa Clara, just north of San Jose. There are shows and an IMAX movie theater as well, and when you need a break, you can ride the antique Ameri-Go-Round.

Better wait until after the roller coasters for lunch!

Do your own experiments downstairs in the Wizard's Lab.

While you're on the campus, stop at the Hall of Health and find out how many calories you can burn in one minute on a stationary bicycle. You'll learn a lot about your body here.

Down the hill, the city of Berkeley is a fun place to people

❧ Jack London ❧

Before he was 30, Jack London was a world-famous author and reporter. Raised in Oakland, he'd gone to Alaska during the 1889 Alaskan Gold Rush, sailed the Pacific, and covered wars.

He was even an oyster pirate along Oakland's waterfront. London, who dropped out of school as a young teenager, loved books and haunted the Oakland Public Library. He taught himself history, politics, and science, all the while writing stories and magazine articles.

London was one of the most popular authors of his day, publishing some 50 books and many short stories and articles. Kids and adults still enjoy his classic adventure stories such as *Sea Wolf*, *White Fang*, and *Call of the Wild*.

Jack London was only 40 when he died.

watch. Your parents will remember that Berkeley was at the center of the protest movement during the Vietnam War. You can still see protesters here (look around Sproul Plaza).

Check out the merchandise, too. Street vendors on Telegraph Avenue sell all kinds of things you won't find in a mall—buttons and beaded jewelry and bumper stickers.

Head to Tilden Regional Park to ride the merry-go-round, the steam train, or the ponies. Swim in Lake Anza or go for a hike. Bring a picnic.

For more water action, the Berkeley Marina is the place. You can walk into the middle of the bay on the 3,000-foot-long pier. On

 Marine World Africa USA

This is the place to go if you want to talk to the animals—from sharks to elephants to exotic birds to dolphins.

Marine World Africa USA is a 160-acre wildlife park and oceanarium that's near the Wine Country in Vallejo, about 30 miles north of San Francisco.

Play tug-of-war with an elephant. Feed a giraffe. Walk through a clear tunnel and watch the sharks swim around you. Look for the trainers working out with tigers.

Watch the sea lions and chimps perform their stunts. Or ride an elephant. See more than 500 butterflies flit around the trees as you walk through their habitat.

Make sure there's plenty of time for the gigantic playground—it's a winner.

weekends and holidays, play in the Adventure Playground. Don't forget your Frisbee.

If you're curious about the Gold Rush or the 1906 earthquake, you'll find out about those events and more at the Oakland Museum. This place is devoted to California history, nature, and art. A great park—Lake Merritt—is nearby.

Many families visiting the Bay Area like to head north from Berkeley and Oakland into the Sonoma and Napa Valley Wine Country. Your parents may like to taste wine, and you'll find plenty to do, too. Learn how wine starts with grapes and ends up in a

FACT:

More than 2 million tons of grapes are crushed in California each year to make wine. Californians have been growing grapes for more than 150 years—680,000 acres worth today. Grapes are one of the state's top cash crops.

bottle. Do you know that the grapes of one vine are enough to make 4 bottles of wine?

Feed the ducks at Sonoma Plaza or ride Traintown's miniature railroad. Have a picnic at Jack London State Historic Park and learn more about the author of much-loved adventure tales at the House of Happy Walls.

There are plenty of parks in the Napa Valley, too, including the Robert Louis Stevenson State Park in Calistoga, complete with the ruins of a mine. Stop at the Silverado Museum to find out all about Stevenson's life.

FACT:

Calistoga's Old Faithful Geyser of California erupts about every 40 minutes. Before a big earthquake, the geyser's schedule goes haywire. Now scientists think there may be a connection. They're studying whether the geyser, which shoots water 60 feet into the air, might help predict earthquakes.

See ancient redwoods that have been turned to stone in the Petrified Forest nearby. Swim in a pool that's naturally heated by hot water bubbling up from the earth. Watch the most famous geyser in California erupt. Get up early for a hot-air balloon ride.

You have to leave the wine to the grown-ups, but there's still plenty of fun awaiting you in the Wine Country.

KIDS! TELL YOUR PARENTS:

Parents don't have to make the vacation 100 percent kid-oriented and give up seeing stuff that interests them. The trick is to get everyone involved in the adventure. Have them explain why they want to go to a particular place. Do they want to go to a certain vineyard because they like the wine made there? Do they remember Berkeley from their student days? Vacations can be a lesson in give and take.

For San Jose information, call the San Jose Convention & Visitors Bureau at 800-SAN-JOSE. Call the Children's Discovery Museum at 408-298-5437, and the Tech Museum of Innovation at 408-279-7150. Call the Berkeley Visitor Information Hotline at 510-549-8710, and the Lawrence Hall of Science at 510-642-5132.

The Sonoma Valley Visitors Bureau can help you plan a tour there. Call 707-996-1090 and ask for the new free guide. Call the Napa Valley Conference and Visitors Bureau at 707-226-7459. Ask for their suggestions on things to do with kids.

If your family plans to visit wineries, call first to see if they welcome children. Sterling Vineyards near Calistoga is one that does. The plus there is the tram ride to the hilltop winery. But make sure the tram is running when you plan to visit. Call 707-942-3300. Another good bet might be Rutherford Hill Winery in St. Helena where there are old caves to tour. Call 707-963-1871. Call 707-644-4000 for Marine World information. Ask about the ticket packages that include ferry service from San Francisco.

Call Paramount's Great America at 408-988-1776.

Kids! *Use this page for your stories and drawings!*

MONTEREY AND SANTA CRUZ
FISH, BUTTERFLIES, BOARDWALKS, AND ARCADES

L ook at them go! The frisky sea otters dive, tumble, and play. They're so cute, you'll wish you could go swimming with them.

Watch them from below the water level as they swim in their 2-story home at the Monterey Bay Aquarium. Get nose-to-nose with

FACT:

The entire population of California sea otters is only about 2,200. The population slowly is recovering after being hunted for years. Sea otters have the thickest fur of any mammal in the world—up to a million hairs per square inch.

them up above. Check them out at meal times! That's raw squid and abalone they're eating.

The otters you see here were rescued as abandoned pups and hand-raised by the aquarium staff. They live in a protected home, but with the same plants and animals that wild otters encounter along the California coast.

Outside the building, you may see young wild sea otters in the Great Tide Pool underneath the aquarium decks. These otters lost their mothers. This is their school and temporary home. Otter care specialists swim with them, teaching them the skills they'll need to hunt for food and survive when they return to the bay.

Look in the water for the harbor seals who swim here. Sometimes sea lions sun themselves on the rocks, barking at passing boats. In the winter, you may spot gray whales as they migrate south.

Inside the Aquarium, you can't miss the Kelp Forest exhibit. It's 3 stories high and gives you a diver's glimpse of the spectacular undersea world that thrives in Monterey Bay. Some kelp plants are 100 feet tall. They can grow 1 foot a day. Hundreds of sea creatures call the kelp forest home. Stop at the Kelp Lab and you can feel the kelp yourself, or get a closer look at a tiny resident through a microscope.

Tide Pools

They're rocky pockets by the shore that keep water in when the tide goes out. Some are large and others very small. They're home to an entire community of sea life—anemones, sponges, worms, snails, sea slugs, mussels, crabs, starfish, and sea urchins. Hundreds of different kinds of creatures live here.

Visit the Long Marine Laboratory and Aquarium in Santa Cruz to learn more about tide pools and the scientists who study them. There are plenty of tide pools for you to explore—along the rocky coast at Asilomar Beach in Pacific Grove, for example; at Natural Bridges State Park near Santa Cruz; Pfeiffer Beach near Big Sur State Park; and Point Reyes National Seashore. Low tide is the best time to explore.

Look for the different types of tide pool inhabitants. If you're lucky, you might even see an octopus.

But step carefully. It's slippery. And remember that life clings to almost every rocky surface here. These sea creatures are fragile. Even turning over a rock can hurt a tiny animal not used to the sun. If you handle the animals or rocks, put them back exactly where you found them. Don't take anything home. Even empty shells might provide a home for some animal later.

Most important, always keep one eye on the sea. Waves and tides aren't predictable.

Wherever you wander in the huge Monterey Bay Aquarium, you'll get a new understanding of the world just outside in the bay and the ocean. There are more than 120,000 plants and animals here. The Aquarium's researchers are working hard to learn more about them.

FACT:

The male seahorse carries and gives birth to the young. The female puts her eggs in a pouch on his belly. Imagine a pregnant dad!

Check out the shapes and colors and sizes of the creatures—the delicate moon jellies and constantly changing octopuses; the frogs and turtles, hermit crabs, and anemones. Each is amazing to watch up close.

Visit the 7-gill shark in the tank it shares with lots of other fish. She doesn't attack because she's well fed here! Touch the bat rays in the Bat Ray Petting Pool. Don't worry—their stingers have been clipped. Nearby, explore the Touch Pool. Can you feel that scratchy sea star?

See the silvery anchovies swim around and around in their tank. Walk through the Sandy Shore Aviary and watch the shore birds close-up.

When you're ready to leave the Aquarium, stroll out to Cannery

Row. Buy an ice cream cone or some fudge. As you browse in the shops, imagine what it must have been like when fishermen were everywhere and workers packed and processed sardines in the canneries. Novelist John Steinbeck described Cannery Row as "A poem, a stink, a grating noise."

You can climb around the steam locomotive or slide down the tubes at the Dennis the Menace Playground on Pearl Street. Hank

⤚❧ John Steinbeck ❧⤙

By the time he was a teenager in Salinas, California, John Steinbeck was scribbling stories and entertaining his friends with his tales.

He grew up to become one of the most famous and popular authors in America, but he never stopped being concerned about ordinary people and their troubles.

Steinbeck was raised and later lived in the heart of California's farmland, and he wrote passionately about the lives of migrant laborers and cannery workers, among others.

You may know his story *The Red Pony*. His greatest novel, *The Grapes of Wrath,* told the story of the Joads, who were driven off their Oklahoma land by the 1930s dust storms, and came to California. Steinbeck won the Pulitzer Prize for the novel. It was so controversial when first published that it was banned in some places. Now *The Grapes of Wrath* is recognized as one of the best American novels ever written.

FACT:

Monterey once was the center of a huge sardine canning industry. The smell was awful! It was California's busiest sea port. By the early 1950s, though, the sardines were gone and the canneries began to close. Since then, the old canneries have been restored and turned into stores and restaurants. The Monterey Bay Aquarium is housed in the rebuilt Hovden Cannery building. It was the last cannery to close, in 1972.

Ketcham, who created the Dennis the Menace comic strip, designed the park. Kids think he did a great job.

You and your parents can rent a moped, bike, or surrey and head out on the Monterey Peninsula Recreation Trail along the bay. Head to Fisherman's Wharf to see if you can catch a few fish yourself. You can rent poles and buy bait here. You can also board a whale-watching ship from here or explore the underwater National Marine Sanctuary aboard the *Nautilus,* a semisubmersible ship.

In the heyday of Fisherman's Wharf, boatloads of salmon, tuna, and sardines were unloaded here. Today, the old wooden wharf is home to all kinds of shops, outdoor fish markets, and restaurants that use recipes handed down from generations of fishermen in their families.

Is it time for lunch yet? Pick your own fruits and vegetables

~ Santa Cruz ~

Plop yourself down on the sand at Santa Cruz Beach and build a gigantic sand castle.

When you're done, the Boardwalk is waiting. Here's one National Historic Landmark your parents won't have to talk you into touring. People have been coming here to play for nearly 90 years and kids like it just as much today as they did at the beginning.

There's an arcade and miniature golf, plenty of junk food, 20 big rides, and 7 rides specially designed for small kids. Don't miss the Giant Dipper wooden roller coaster. Built in 1924, it's still the Boardwalk's most popular ride.

For a different kind of adventure, hop aboard the Roaring Camp & Big Trees Narrow Gauge Railroad in nearby Felton. You can ride it through the redwood forest, up a mountain, or down to the Boardwalk. It stops right in front of the carousel, built in 1911. Can you catch a brass ring?

You can also fish or whale watch here. Say hello to the lounging sea lions. They're easy to find. Just look underneath the Municipal Wharf.

north of Monterey. There are kiwis and apples, raspberries, and even pumpkins in the fall. Look for the farm signs.

If you're visiting in the fall or winter, you'll want to stop at Santa Cruz's Natural Bridges State Park or at Pacific Grove, dubbed Butterfly Town U.S.A., to see the swarms of monarch butterflies. Don't be concerned about finding the butterflies; you can't miss them. Thousands come here for the winter. The Pacific Grove Museum of Natural History is a good place to find out more

FACT:

Most migrating birds and whales travel the same route every year. But the tens of thousands of monarch butterflies that migrate to Pacific Grove every winter have never been there before. Several generations have lived and died in the time since last year's butterflies came.

about them. Every fall, kids here dress in butterfly costumes and hold a parade to celebrate the monarchs' return.

KIDS! TELL YOUR PARENTS:

Enjoy California's great beaches, but be careful around the water. The undertows can be fierce and the water cold. Kids shouldn't swim unsupervised or even play on the beach without someone keeping a close eye on them. Many Northern California beaches don't have lifeguards.

Most kids love the beach. Stop at a market and pick up some plastic shovels and pails so everyone can dig and make sand castles. But in the summer, don't spend more than 90 minutes in the sun without a break. Use plenty of sunscreen and drink lots of water. No one wants a painful sunburn to ruin the family vacation.

To plan a visit to the Monterey Peninsula, call the Monterey Peninsula Visitors & Convention Bureau at 408-649-1770. Ask about hotels that offer Aquarium packages. Call the Monterey Bay Aquarium at 408-648-4800 and check what special programs may be offered when you'll be visiting.

For Santa Cruz information, contact the Santa Cruz County Conference and Visitors Council at 408-425-1234. Check the Roaring Camp & Big Trees Narrow Gauge Railroad schedule at 408-335-4484. The Long Marine Laboratory is open only in the afternoon. Call 408-459-4308.

Kids! Use this page for your stories and drawings!

LAKE TAHOE

Crystal-Clear Water, Skis, Mountain Bikes, and Pioneers

The Evil Spirit was chasing the Young Brave and he needed help fast! The Good Spirit gave him a tree branch. "Drop a leaf when the Evil Spirit nears," the Good Spirit instructed. The leaf would form a pond when it touched the ground. The Evil Spirit couldn't swim, so the Brave would be able to escape. But the

Brave panicked and dropped the entire branch. That's the way Lake Tahoe was formed, according to Native American legend.

Scientists tell a far different story. A melting glacier filled Lake Tahoe, they say. The basin itself was formed millions of years earlier.

However Lake Tahoe was formed, it's the perfect playground today. Do you have a couple hours to spare? Take a drive around the lake to see how big it really is. Better yet, go for a cruise on the *Tahoe Queen* paddle-wheeler. Look for the Lake Tahoe monster. Some people swear they've seen something big out there, like the Loch Ness monster. But local experts say it's probably just a wave or a big fish.

There are lots of places to camp. In the summer, kids fish, swim, and hike all day long here. For easy hikes, try the Tahoe Rim Trail. Or head into the huge Tahoe National Forest. Many people like the Vikingsholm Trail to Emerald Bay. If you like castles, stop to see the Vikingsholm Castle in the summer.

FACT:

Lake Tahoe holds more than 39 trillion gallons of water—enough to cover the entire state of California with more than 14 inches of water. That's sufficient drinking water to supply every person in the United States for 5 years. The lake is 12 miles wide, 22 miles long, 72 miles around, and more than 1,600 feet deep in some places.

Take a picnic and ride Squaw Valley's tram, 8,200 feet up the mountain. The lake certainly looks different from up there.

Bring your mountain bike (or rent one here). Several ski areas, such as Northstar-at-Tahoe and Squaw Valley, have become popular summer mountain bike parks, with miles of challenging trails up and down the ski slopes.

The Donner Party

The families set out from Missouri in 1846 in high spirits. Led by the Donners, their wagons were bursting with supplies. The sun was shining. The 14 children along were excited. They were on their way to settle in California—the adventure of their lives.

Less than half of the 87 migrators lived to finish the trip. The trouble started when they opted for a short cut. They got terribly lost. They had to cut a road through the mountains. Most of their oxen died crossing the 80-mile-wide Great Salt Lake Desert.

By the time the exhausted group got to the Sierra Nevada in October, there was already too much snow for them to go on. They camped near what is now Donner Lake. Some left to seek help, but they couldn't get back until months later.

Many in the Donner Party starved to death. Those who survived were forced to resort to cannibalism. You can hear more about their sad story at the Emigrant Trail Museum in Donner Memorial State Park. Even better, hike the Emigrant Trail, the route they covered.

The Donners and those with them have become a symbol of the pioneers' spirit and courage.

There's plenty of room to bike on flat ground, too. Could you make it 72 miles around the lake? Donner Lake offers nice bike trails, too.

Take some time to look around at the flowers—white ranger buttons, yellow buttercups, and blue asters. How many different ones can you name?

Go bird watching, or hunt for animal tracks. You also can ride horses or play miniature golf.

Roam around Truckee for an afternoon. The Western America Ski & Sport Museum is the place to find out about the history of skiing. At the Emigrant Trail Museum in Donner Memorial Park, you can find out more about the pioneers who struggled across the mountains here in their covered wagons. There are lots of shops, too, including an outlet mall.

If you're looking for water action, you won't

FACT:

Miners were the first skiers in California. During the 1849 Gold Rush, Norwegian immigrants taught the snowbound miners how to strap long wooden boards on their boots and glide over the snow. The idea caught on fast.

FACT:

The water in Lake Tahoe is so clear that objects can be seen plainly even 120 feet below the surface. It looks so blue because the clear water reflects the sky. But it's cold—only 68 degrees in the summer.

be disappointed.
You can water-ski,
kayak, sail, swim
all day long, and take a cruise during
dinner. But be careful—the water can be
really cold. When you get tired, there's
plenty of beach for lounging. In the
winter, there's snow. There's so much of
it that people ski here through the
spring. They also go snowmobiling,
cross-country skiing, sleigh riding, and
ice-skating.

FACT:

Forty feet of snow—some-
times more—falls around
Lake Tahoe every year. That's
why so many skiers come
here. Look for snowboarders
racing down the slopes as
well. Snowboarding is the
hot new winter sport—
especially for teens.

✤ Gold! ✤

James Marshall spotted the sparkling yellow flakes in a stream. Gold!

That January morning in 1848, he rushed to tell his boss, John Sutter. They had been building a sawmill at the edge of the American River at Sutter's Fort.

Soon the word was out. No one had ever seen anything like this. The Gold Rush was on! Thousands of men raced to the rugged foothills of the Sierra Nevada from all over the world to join the hunt for gold. They became known as *forty-niners* because most of them came in 1849. Entire families pulled up stakes to follow the men.

Few struck it rich panning for gold in the icy streams. Life was very hard. Most stopped mining within a few years to farm, raise families, open stores, or start businesses. They changed California forever.

Got gold fever? You can look for some in California's Gold Country. Try Placer County. Don't forget your mining pan.

If you're a skier or want to learn, this is the spot. Many of the mountains here offer special programs for kids. Programs at Squaw Valley and Northstar-at-Tahoe are among the best. In addition, Tahoe Handicapped Ski School at Alpine Meadows teaches skiing to adults and kids with disabilities.

Have you ever raced down a mountain on skis? Watch out for the trees.

FACT:

The 1960 Winter Olympics were held at Squaw Valley. That was the first time Olympic events were broadcast daily on television.

～ ...and Silver! ～

The prospectors were looking for gold when they stumbled on silver in 1859—the biggest discovery of silver ore ever.

The Comstock Lode sparked a new rush to the hills, helped finance the Union's Civil War effort, paid for some of San Francisco's biggest buildings, and built Virginia City in Nevada. The silver was found there about 40 miles from the south shore of Lake Tahoe. Bonanza Road, the first west-to-east road across the mountains, was built for those hurrying back and forth to the mines.

Soon dubbed "The Richest Place on Earth," Virginia City in its heyday was the biggest city between St. Louis and San Francisco. Today, fewer than 1,000 people live in this Nevada town close to the California border. But with its old buildings, wooden sidewalks, and mining lore, California kids say it's a great place to get a taste of those rough-and-tumble days.

KIDS! TELL YOUR PARENTS:

Skiing is a great family sport, but only if everyone wants to ski. Invest in some lessons to get everyone started. It's very difficult for parents to teach their kids. Make sure everyone has appropriate clothing—weatherproof pants, gloves and jackets, heavy socks, hats and sweaters. There's nothing like soggy mittens or freezing ears to ruin a day on the slopes.

If kids don't want to ski, they shouldn't be forced. Whatever you're doing, if you're not used to high altitudes, take it slowly at first and give everyone in the family time to adjust. Drink extra water to avoid headaches.

Ski resorts offer lots of special deals and packages for families. But make sure to ask about them when you book your reservations, not after you arrive.

Most importantly, make sure your car is ready for the snowy mountain roads. You can rent a 4-wheel-drive vehicle, or bring chains for your own car. The driving around Lake Tahoe in the winter can be beautiful but very difficult. Be careful!

For information about the South Shore of Lake Tahoe, call 800-AT-TAHOE. For information about the North Shore, call 800-824-6348. Call the Placer County Visitor Information Center at 916-887-2111 to find out about places to pan for gold. Call the Virginia City Visitors' Bureau at 702-847-0177.

For Lake Tahoe-area national forest recreation information call 800-280-CAMP. For more information about the Donner Memorial Park and the Emigrant Trail Museum, call 916-582-7892.

Kids! *Use this page for your stories and drawings!*

YOSEMITE NATIONAL PARK
WATERFALLS, GIANT TREES, BEARS, AND RAINBOWS

Ready to get soaked? That's what happens when you hike next to the waterfalls. In fact, some say the spirits who live at Bridalveil Fall get their kicks from drenching everyone who comes close.

It's worth getting wet to see Yosemite National Park's falls up close. They're fantastic! It's rare to see so many waterfalls so close together. If you visit in the spring, they're especially strong. The amount of water is directly related to how much snow has fallen in the winter.

It's an easy walk to the base of Bridalveil Fall and Yosemite Falls, but a tough 7-mile hike to Nevada Fall and back down. Many families opt to head up the Mist Trail to the top of Vernal Fall. It's easy until you pass Vernal Fall Bridge. Don't be fooled because it's only a little more than a mile to the top—it's straight uphill. Little kids might have a tough time making it. But if you can do it, you won't forget hiking right alongside a rushing waterfall.

Be careful! The rocks are slippery close to the falls. Look for the rainbows. You'll see them over the waterfalls when the sun is shining. When there's a big, bright full moon, you

FACT:

Half Dome rises 4,800 feet above the eastern end of Yosemite Valley. Here's the Native American legend that explains how it was formed: A young Indian couple came to Yosemite. When they got to the spot that is now Mirror Lake, they began to argue. She ran away. He chased her. Because they brought anger into Yosemite, they were turned to stone. He became North Dome and she Half Dome. She began to cry and her tears filled Mirror Lake. Can you find the marks of her tears on the rock?

might see "moonbows" over the falls.

Yosemite is a great place for kids—and parents. It's huge: 250 miles of roads and 800 miles of hiking trails wind through this park.

In the winter, a lot of California kids come to ski at Badger Pass and play in the snow. The rest of the year, families camp, hike, and fish for trout here. The water is cold but you can swim in the summer. Never swim upstream of waterfalls, though.

If you prefer to stay dry, the park offers horseback riding and miles of biking trails. You can rent a bike—and a helmet—or sign up for a trail ride if you're at least 7.

One good ride or easy hike is out to Mirror Lake. It's the best place to see Half Dome, Yosemite's famous rounded cliff. In the summer, you'll see rock climbers making their ascent. Eat a picnic lunch while you watch them climb. They move pretty slowly but you would too if you were 1,000 feet up in the air.

FACT:

Yosemite Falls is the tallest waterfall in North America—2,425 feet. Lower Fall alone is twice the height of Niagara Falls.

FACT:

Native Americans lived in Yosemite for about 4,000 years before the Gold Rush. The Miwok tribe named the valley "Ahwahnee," which means "place of a gaping mouth."

You'll see lots of animals here, and, if you visit when they're in bloom, big fields of brightly colored wildflowers. Can you see the strange red plant on the forest floor that has no leaves at all? It's called a *snowplant,* probably because it appears just after the snow melts. There are more than 1,400 kinds of flowering plants in the park. See how many different ones you can find.

Bears

Black bears really are brown. Some 300 of them roam the park. You won't see a grizzly. There aren't any here anymore.

Bears who get used to eating our food lose their fear of people. They can get aggressive when they decide to look for food. Bears can hurt people who get in the animals' way or scare them.

Never approach a bear, regardless of its size. If you see one, yell, clap your hands, or throw objects—from a safe distance—to scare it away. Never feed a bear, either. If you're camping, keep food in air-tight containers so the bears can't smell it.

Look for bighorn sheep and red-tailed hawks in the mountains, mule deer (they get their name from their big ears), chipmunks, coyotes, lots of birds, and, of course, black bears. At night, listen for the hoots of the great horned owl.

Stop at the Visitor Center (check out the reconstructed Indian Village of the Ahwahnee behind the building) or, in the summer, the Happy Isles Nature Center, and ask about the Explorer Packs for kids. Available in spring and summer, they're stuffed with guidebooks and activities that will make your time at Yosemite more fun as you watch birds, hunt for rocks, or look at the giant

 Animal Smarts

There are more than 80 mammal and nearly 250 bird species at Yosemite. Some are not often seen. To spot animals as you hike, here are some tips from Yosemite rangers:

- Wear darker colors so you don't stand out.
- Head away from the crowds.
- Watch for dens, trails, or holes marked by pine nuts or acorns.
- If you see an animal, move slowly so you don't scare it.
- Stop moving and watch from a distance.
- Don't approach the animals. They're wild!
- Never feed the animals.

trees and tiny forest creatures.

You might want to become a junior ranger, or, if you're 11 or 12, a senior ranger. Go to a family campfire one evening or join a ranger's hike. The ranger will be able to answer all your questions. LeConte Memorial, which opens in May, has all kinds of special summer programs for kids, as does Tuolumne Meadows.

❧ Hiking Smarts ❧

Be careful out there. Here are some common-sense ranger rules to keep you safe on the trail:

- Wear sturdy, comfortable shoes.
- Stay on the trail. Not only can you damage the habitat, but hiking off the trail also increases your chances of getting hurt—or lost.
- Never hike alone, and make sure you keep track of one another. Wait at trail turns.
- Always carry rain gear and a jacket, food, and water. Don't drink the water in the rivers and streams. It might be contaminated.
- Wear sunscreen.
- If someone in your family becomes hurt or injured, send someone ahead for help. Write down your exact location as well as the age, size, and weight of the injured person so the rangers will be able to bring the right kind of help.
- Stash a flashlight and a small first aid kit in your pack.

FACT:

Giant sequoias are the largest living things on earth. The Grizzly Giant is 209 feet tall and 31 feet around in circumference. At 2,700 years old, it's one of the oldest living sequoias and the largest in the Mariposa Grove.

Another place with kids' programs is the Pioneer Yosemite History Center, at the south end of the park near the Wawona Hotel. Visit the furnished cabins from different eras in Yosemite's history. How would you like to be locked up in their tiny jail?

During the summer, volunteers dress in costumes and portray early Yosemite residents. Watch the blacksmith work. Can you shoe a horse?

Eco-Cool

Here are some ways rangers say you can help protect beautiful places like Yosemite and improve the environment at home, too:

• Brush your teeth using a minimum of water.
• Pick up litter when you see it—even if it's not yours.
• Turn off the lights when they're not being used.
• Use rechargeable batteries. Throw-away batteries are really hard on the environment.
• Don't buy things with a lot of packaging.
• Plant a tree in your yard.

Stop at the the nearby Mariposa Grove of giant sequoias. You've probably never seen such gigantic trees, even at Muir Woods. You can hike through the grove or, in the summer, take an open tram. You can see the Grizzly Giant and the California Tunnel Tree, with a huge tunnel carved through it.

Thousands and thousands of visitors went through the famous Wawona Tunnel Tree—on horses, in stagecoaches, and later, in cars.

FACT:

Giant sequoias have thick trunks and gigantic branches. Their cousins, the coast redwoods, are taller, thinner, and have darker brown trunks.

But all that traffic ultimately weakened the tree's root system and it fell. You can still see it lying in the grove.

You also can walk through a tree at the Tuolumne Grove of Big Trees. Here you'll find the Dead Giant, the last drive-through tree in the park.

Don't leave Yosemite without stopping at Glacier Point. (In the winter, you can get there only on snowshoes!) This is the place to see all of Yosemite Valley. Stay to see the moon rise. And don't forget your camera.

FACT:

Yosemite Valley is one of the most amazing examples anywhere of the power of glaciers. Their grinding, gouging force is what carved the valley into its U-shape.

⇜ Scale Those Rocks! ⇝

Here are some words rock climbers use all the time:
- RAPPELLING—Descending a rock face on a rope.
- BELAYING—Holding the safety rope or letting it out for another climber.
- BOLT—A device drilled into rock to anchor a rope.
- PROTECTION—Any device that is used to limit the length of a fall.
- CARABINER—A link that allows you to clip your rope to a bolt or other climbing equipment.

KIDS! TELL YOUR PARENTS:

If the family is going hiking or camping, be prepared. Kids often get bored and hungry on the trail, so plan shorter hikes and always have a supply of snacks and water. Try singing songs or organizing a scavenger hunt when the kids decide they've hiked far enough. Hikes are the perfect time to tell some of those embarrassing old family stories.

In the summer, Yosemite is very crowded. You must call ahead for reservations—don't come without any. Camping reservations can be made 8 weeks before your visit. You'll have more fun if you plan your visit beforehand. What do you want to see? What trails would you like to hike? Check ahead to see which programs are offered on the days you plan to visit: Different activities are offered on different days. Don't try to do too much. You can't possibly see the entire park, so relax and enjoy what you can see.

For reservation information, call 209-252-4848. For camping reservations, call 800-365-2267. Dinner or breakfast at the historic Ahwahnee Hotel is a real treat, and reservations are a must for dinner. Call 209-372-1489. For general park information, call 209-372-0264.

To help you plan, the Yosemite Association Bookstore sells a variety of books. Consider *The Complete Guidebook to Yosemite National Park,* by Steven P. Medley ($10.95) and *Easy Day Hikes in Yosemite,* by Deborah J. Durkee ($4.50). Call 209-379-2648 to order.

Kids! Use this page for your stories and drawings!